EARTH
in Motion

by Christian Downey

PEARSON

Scott
Foresman

How Earth Moves

Earth is always moving. In fact, Earth is spinning as you read this. Why can't you feel it? You are moving with Earth. When Earth spins, everything on it spins too. Earth's movement is smooth and steady.

How do you know Earth is moving? One way you can tell is that the Sun and the stars seem to be moving in the sky. Another way is by observing the change in seasons. This change is more obvious in some places than in others. The change in seasons is partly due to how Earth moves through space.

Scientists use many types of equipment to see how objects seem to move in the sky.

Earth as seen from space

The Rotation of Earth

Earth spins around its axis. The **axis** is an imaginary line that goes through Earth from the North Pole to the South Pole. A **rotation** is the spinning of Earth around its axis. One complete turn around the axis is one rotation. It takes Earth almost twenty-four hours, or one day, to make a full rotation.

Earth spins from west to east, but objects in the sky appear to move from east to west. You can see why this happens with a simple experiment. Hold your hand in front of your face. Move your head to the right. Did you notice that your hand seemed to move to the left? This is how the movement of the Sun and other stars appears to people on Earth. Earth moves from west to east, and the Sun and other stars appear to move from east to west.

The Sun appears to move through the sky during the day.

Shadows

In the morning and evening, when the Sun seems low in the sky, shadows look long. In the middle of the day, when the Sun appears to be overhead, shadows look short. Earth's rotation also causes day to become night and night to become day. Any place that is turned toward the Sun experiences daytime. Nighttime is when that part of Earth is turned away from the Sun.

The Sun shines too brightly for us to see stars during the day. Look at a clear sky for several nights. You may notice that stars seem to move from east to west in the sky.

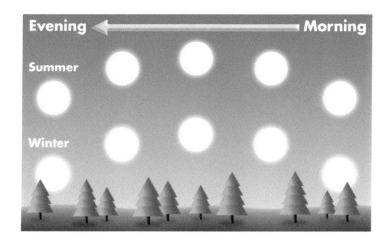

Daylight

Every place on Earth has a different number of daylight hours at different times of the year. This chart shows the changes in daylight hours over a year, in Chicago, a city in the Northern Hemisphere.

Hours of Daylight in Chicago

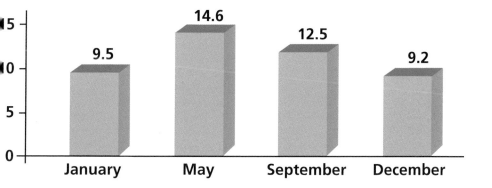

Revolutions of Earth

Earth rotates on its axis. It also revolves around the Sun at the same time. A **revolution** is the movement of one object around another. Earth has made one revolution when it has made one full trip around the Sun. An **orbit** is the path Earth takes around the Sun.

Earth completes one full revolution around the Sun in about 365 days, or one year. Earth travels a long distance at a fast speed during that time! Earth travels a total of about 940,000,000 kilometers in a year. It moves at a speed of about 107,000 kilometers per hour.

The sizes and distances in this diagram are not true to scale.

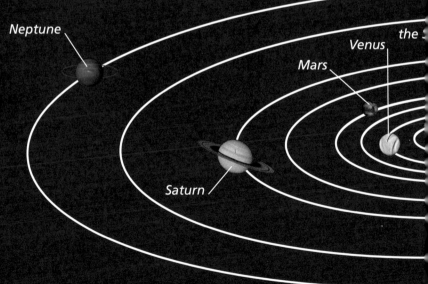

Neptune

Saturn

Mars

Venus

the

The orbit of Earth is an ellipse. An **ellipse** is a sort of stretched-out circle. Earth's distance from the Sun changes at different parts of its orbit. Sometimes Earth is farther from the Sun than at other times. Sometimes it is close.

Gravity pulls two objects together. It can work from far away. Gravity is the force that keeps Earth revolving around the Sun. Earth would move out into space if gravity did not keep it in place. Gravity would cause Earth and the Sun to crash into each other if Earth stopped moving.

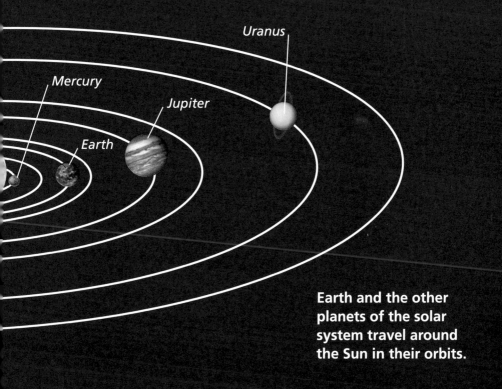

Uranus

Mercury

Jupiter

Earth

Earth and the other planets of the solar system travel around the Sun in their orbits.

Earth's Axis

Earth's axis is always tilted in the same direction. This tilt means that different areas on Earth get direct sunlight at different places in the orbit.

Earth can be divided into two halves, the Northern and Southern Hemispheres. When one hemisphere is tilted toward the Sun, the other is tilted away. The hemisphere that is tilted toward the Sun has warmer weather and longer days. It is summer there. While that half of Earth is warm, the other half is colder. It is winter in the other hemisphere. Earth's axis is not tilted toward or away from the Sun during spring or fall. During spring and fall in both hemispheres, the weather is less extreme. Hours of daylight and nighttime are more balanced.

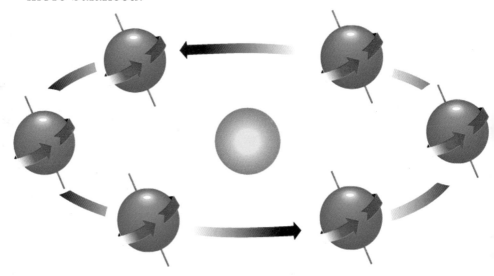

Different hemispheres tilt toward the Sun at different points in Earth's orbit.

When it is winter in the United States...

...it is summer in Australia.

The Southern Hemisphere is tilted toward the Sun during part of the year. It gets more direct sunlight. That means it gets more heat. Temperatures there are higher, and it is summer. While the Southern Hemisphere is tilted toward the Sun, the Northern Hemisphere is tilted away from the Sun. It gets less direct sunlight. So it gets less heat and has lower temperatures. It is winter. That means that while it is winter in the United States, it is summer in Australia! Temperatures in the spring and fall are milder in both hemispheres.

Patterns in the Sky

The Moon is the easiest object to see in the night sky. The Moon appears to shine brightly. But the Moon's light comes from sunlight reflecting off its surface. The Sun acts as a light bulb, and the Moon acts as a mirror.

The Moon orbits Earth. The Moon's orbit, just like Earth's orbit, is an ellipse. There is gravity between the Moon and Earth. This holds the Moon in its orbit. The Moon's revolution around Earth takes a little longer than twenty-seven days.

The Moon turns around its own axis as it circles Earth. As it rotates one time on its axis, it also revolves one time around Earth. Because of this, the same side of the Moon always faces Earth.

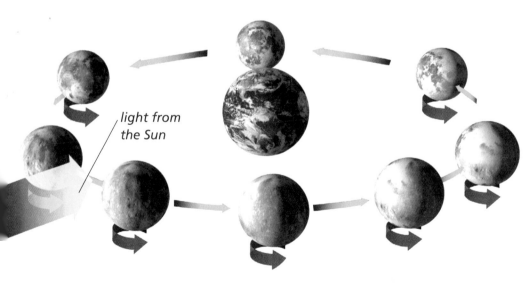

light from the Sun

The Moon spins around on its axis as it revolves around Earth.

The Moon's Phases

The Moon appears to be different shapes at different times of the month. Only half of the Moon ever faces the Sun. Sunlight reflects on the surface of that half. A full Moon appears when the lighted half faces Earth directly.

Most of the time, we see only part of the lighted half of the Moon. The different shapes that the Moon seems to have are called phases of the Moon. Each phase lasts a short time. A set of phases begins with a new Moon. This is when the part of the Moon facing Earth cannot be seen. It is followed by a crescent. This is a sliver of lighted Moon. Then a larger part of the Moon is visible. We call this the first quarter. Soon the entire half of the Moon is visible. This full Moon appears as a full circle. After that we see the Moon in the phase called the last quarter. It looks similar to a half circle. The phases begin again with the new Moon.

crescent Moon

first quarter Moon

full Moon

last quarter Moon

Eclipses

An eclipse happens when one object in space comes between the Sun and another object and casts its shadow on the other object. This happens when the Moon crosses Earth's shadow, or when the Moon's shadow reaches part of Earth.

A lunar eclipse occurs when the Moon passes directly through Earth's shadow. This can only happen when the Moon is full. The Moon and the Sun must also be on opposite sides of Earth for this to happen. During a lunar eclipse, Earth blocks all or part of the Sun's rays from reaching the Moon.

A partial eclipse happens when only part of the Moon is in Earth's shadow. Not every place on Earth can see every eclipse. A lunar eclipse is only visible from the places on Earth where it is night.

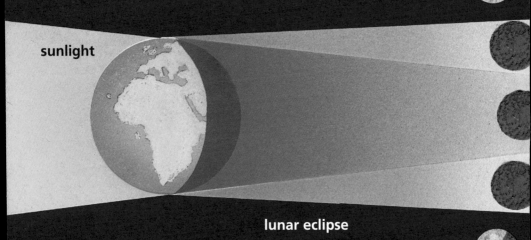

sunlight

lunar eclipse

During a solar eclipse, the Moon blocks the Sun from view.

A solar eclipse occurs when the Moon passes between the Sun and Earth and casts its shadow on Earth. The Moon may block part or all of the Sun from view. When the Moon blocks the Sun, a shadow is cast. But the shadow covers only a small part of Earth. A solar eclipse can only be seen from the places on Earth that are in Moon's shadow.

A solar eclipse is an amazing sight. However, it is never safe to look straight at the Sun. Any direct sunlight can damage your eyes, even causing blindness.

Stars

Scientists think there may be 1 billion trillion stars in the universe. That would be a 1 followed by 21 zeroes! That's a lot of stars! The Sun is the star closest to Earth. It gives Earth light and energy. Some stars are bigger and hotter than the Sun. Other stars are smaller and cooler.

The brightness of the Sun keeps us from seeing stars during the day. If stars are very far away, they may not seem as bright. You can see more stars with a telescope than you can with just your eyes.

Constellations

Some stars seem to form patterns. Scientists call each of these star patterns a **constellation.** Astronomers have divided the sky into eighty-eight constellations. Stars are often identified by the constellations they are in. Although stars may appear close together within a constellation, they may be very far apart.

The constellation Scorpio forms the shape of a scorpion.

Because of Earth's rotation, stars appear to move through the sky in a straight line at the equator. Near the North and South Poles, stars appear to move in circles. The stars that can be seen in the Northern Hemisphere are different from the stars seen in the Southern Hemisphere. Polaris, or the North Star, is visible in the sky over the North Pole.

Eclipses and constellations make our sky fun to watch and learn about. Scientists continue to learn new things about Earth, the Sun, and the Moon. Years from now, people on Earth will look at the same sky but may know much more about it than we do now.

Glossary

axis   an imaginary line that goes through Earth's center

constellation   a group of stars in the sky that seem to form a pattern

eclipse   the passing of an object in space between the Sun and another object

ellipse   a stretched-out circle

lunar eclipse   the passing of the Moon directly through Earth's shadow

orbit   the path Earth follows as it revolves around the Sun

revolution   the movement of one object around another

rotation   the spinning of Earth around its axis

solar eclipse   the passing of the Moon between the Sun and Earth